P9-CFO-148

Strong Survival:
The Life and Times of a Mountain Woman

by Cliffie Strong
with
photography & CAP
Perspectives by Ike Adams

Strong family photographs used
with permission of the Strong family

CHRISTIAN APPALACHIAN PROJECT

First Edition

Printed in the United States of America

© 2004 Christian Appalachian Project | All Rights Reserved

4606-9

Table of Contents

Dear Friend of CAP,

I'm so pleased and proud to send you this wonderful book about the life of Cliffie Strong. I think you will find it uplifting and amazing. In addition to reading about her courage and faith, you'll also learn more about CAP's programs and our many efforts to relieve the suffering in this poverty-stricken region. I hope you'll feel good knowing that your donation helps to support all we do on behalf of the people of Appalachia.

Thank you, and enjoy reading!

Sue Sword

Sue Sword
Vice President

Prologue

During the early nineties, Naomi McIntosh, a Christian Appalachian Project (CAP) staff person, began providing basic visitation, transportation services and socialization opportunities to lonely, isolated, elderly people in Owsley County, Kentucky.

Because of Owsley County's exceptionally remote geographic location, CAP had not previously spent a lot of time there. Traveling to Owsley County required negotiating narrow, winding and dangerously steep mountain roads to reach a population that numbered only 5,106.

CAP was diligently trying to spread its relatively scant resources into communities where they would reach the greatest numbers of people suffering from poverty. The goal was to provide relief to the neediest of the needy and, at the same time, serve the greatest number of people possible.

For the most part, CAP worked in more accessible counties with population bases five or six times greater than the population of Owsley County. Poverty rates in those counties were staggering enough and more people were in dire straits than CAP could possibly reach at one time.

But along with population data, the 1990 Census also provided hard information that showed Owsley to be the poorest county in the state, and the seventh poorest in the nation when such things as income and unemployment levels were considered. A larger percentage (more than half) of the population lived below the poverty level than almost any place else in the nation. CAP also discovered that chief among those suffering the cruelest poverty was Owsley County's disproportionate number of elderly people.

Since its very beginning, CAP has offered compassion to the region's elderly people. Taking the forms of simple companionship, basic transportation for groceries and medical attention, organized social/spiritual events, and simple assurance that someone cared about them, CAP has replaced loneliness and despair with hope and joy for countless isolated and lonely elderly people as they wind down their years on earth.

In Cliffie Strong, Naomi found a remarkable, surviving victim of central Appalachia's harsh and unforgiving circumstances. She also found in Cliffie, the treasures of wisdom, talent and dogged determination that only a relative few mountain women have used to reach Cliffie's age. These skills were naturally and necessarily developed to scrape by and somehow survive the punishing social/economic environment of rural, central Appalachia.

All too often, Appalachia's elderly are widows or widowers left to get by on their own devices. Even in their seventies and eighties, they may go for days without any real contact with another human being. Frequently they can't afford phone service. Their children are often several states away, struggling themselves, and unable to provide more than a pittance of financial support. Nursing homes or retirement communities are far beyond their means. CAP simply fills a void in their lives. As you will discover in this book, Naomi McIntosh bridged a deep and debilitating void in the life of Cliffie Strong.

Cliffie and Naomi bonded almost like kin. Now 88 years old, Cliffie wants to tell her story about what it was like to grow up in the mountains of eastern Kentucky. CAP is elated with the opportunity to enable her to do just that.

Because Cliffie has mostly benefited from just one or two CAP Programs, "perspective" chapters are interspersed throughout her story. The intent is to enable readers to not only understand what life was like in the mountains through most of the last century, but also to tell you about the modern role CAP plays in helping Appalachia's people overcome a host of social and economic barriers.

Cliffie's story is a straightforward and powerful presentation of both historic and current reality in central Appalachia. Be forewarned that her grammar may not always be as precise as that to which you are normally accustomed and she may leave you scratching your head when you don't always grasp her terminology. But this is Cliffie's story as she told it to us in the winter of 2003-2004. It contains history, wisdom and wit. It may make you laugh on one page and weep a bit on the next.

Rest assured that you will be enlightened and entertained. More importantly, you will understand, when you reach the end of the book, why Cliffie believes it to be so important.

Enjoy!

Cliffie works on her quilts

Chapter 1

Cliffie's Story
(born in the hills of home)

I am an old mountain woman.

My name is Cliffie Strong and I am 88 years of age.

I was born into God's beautiful world, in a cabin deep in the heart of the Appalachian Mountains, on the fifth day of October 1915 in Jackson County, Kentucky on Big Sturgeon Creek, right near the Owsley County line. I have lived out my life on poor old hillside farms, within a few miles of my birthplace, and I've scratched out a living off the land as best I could these many years. My proudest accomplishment is that I have survived many hard times.

I know that most people don't live to be near as old as I am and most of those who do can't get around as well as I do now. But my mind is as keen as it ever was and hardly a day goes by that I don't learn something new.

A few months back, some of my dear and wonderful friends at the Christian Appalachian Project offered to let me tell the story of my life and put it in print. I'm not much of a hand at writing anymore but I can talk up a storm. So I'm just going to talk and let somebody else take it all down and write it up. I'm tickled to pieces, and thankful for the opportunity to tell about my life so that the younger generation might have a record of what it was like to live out a life that covers most of the 20th Century in our dear old hills of home. I also want to let you know what a lifesaving thing CAP has been to me and I ask you to pray for both me and CAP as you read my story.

I hope I can give you some sound advice from lessons I have learned the hard way and I hope that I can make you grin a little if you don't laugh out loud. What a sad and lonesome place this world would be if we didn't take a little time to laugh at ourselves every now and then.

I also hope that I can make you do some sober thinking about how hard life can be and how to make do when nobody else is going to do for you. And then I will tell you how wonderful it is when The Good Lord sends angels into your life to help you out when you can't stand alone, but more of that later. Let's get on with my story.

I had 12 full brothers and sisters and 12 half-brothers and sisters and most of them were born before me. My Dad was Isaac Shelby Bowles. He had been married before and his wife died giving birth to their thirteenth child.

Cliffie's father,
Isaac Shelby Bowles

A couple of years later, he married my mother, Callie Jane Lorton. She must have been about the youngest one of her family, and together they had 12 children though three of them died at birth or infancy. All told, my Dad fathered 25 children.

Mother was actually 22 years younger than my Dad and to this day I don't know why she married him. She was a beautiful, well-built woman and she kept her looks until she was in her old age. I think she could have had any man she wanted.

By the time I came along, most of my older half brothers and sisters were already grown and scattered out with families of their own. I was the sixth child of Dad's second family so by the time I was old enough to begin remembering much, the older ones were not around very often and

Cliffie's mother (on right)
Callie Jane (Lorton) Bowles

none of them lived in our household.

This actually was not uncommon in the mountains back then. People married young and many men raised families by two or three women and it was not because of a divorce. In fact, divorce was considered immoral and it was almost unheard of.

Women tended to have a lot of children because little or nothing was known about family planning and besides that, the more children you had, the more help you had in keeping up a homestead. But all that child bearing and raising took its toll. On average a child was born about every two years and trouble during childbirth was the leading cause of death among women.

If it wasn't problems with labor, it was infections that set in and led to death soon after the birth. All babies were born at home and rarely did they involve a doctor. Midwives who had hand-me-down training from older women of past generations took care of the birthing. Both my mother and my grandmother on my mother's side of the family were respected midwives.

You can go to old graveyards and see on the tombstones where many women died when they were in their thirties and forties while the men lived to ripe old ages. Of course today, women tend to outlive men. Somewhere along the way I guess we just got smarter. Of course improvements in medicine helped a lot too.

Our hills were not populated to speak of at the turn of the century. One family might own one holler and just over the ridge a different family would own another and so forth. Generally each family owned large tracts of land consisting of hundreds of acres of rugged hillsides that were actually too steep to do much with in the way of growing crops but gradually we cleared off enough land to raise whatever we needed to keep us going.

So it may have been a mile or more to the closest neighbor and the only way you could get there was to walk or ride a nag. Grown-ups could ride a mule or horse, but when I was little you had to walk barefooted if you wanted to get from one place to another. Except in the winter, and even then you went barefooted unless there was a snow on the ground or it was froze so hard you just couldn't get around without something on your feet.

So that's how we got about. We mostly walked barefooted and I can't remember that ever bothering me much. Your feet got used to it and you just went on because it was natural. Bout the worse thing that could happen was when you stumped your big toe against a rock or a root and it would swell up and you had to limp a little. Or if you stepped on a bee or yellow jacket and got stung in the soft part there in the arch of your foot.

You might get cut with a tool like an ax or saw or a mowing blade, while you were working. Or you might fall down and scrape your knee or elbow or you might get scratched real deep with a thorn or get burned from a hot cinder out of the fireplace. There was any number of ways that you could get cut or blistered and it would set up infection and they would turn into something that wouldn't heal unless you took care of them pretty fast.

We made our own healing salve. It consisted of one part pine tree resin that clumped up on the tree trunks, and one part mutton tallow which is the grease that cooks off lamb or sheep meat. We added some petroleum jelly when we could find it to make it thinner or some hog lard. We also added some black poplar buds which we called Balm of Gilead in the spring. Heat the whole thing up until it melted together, stir it up good and let it set until it thickened up and you had a salve that would heal about any sore you got. Man or beast, it drew the infection out and kept it from getting in. To this day I don't know why that recipe has not been patented because it worked better than about anything you can buy in a drug store these days and it didn't cost a dime.

And, of course, we used all manner of herbs and roots to make tonics for internal ailments but anymore, I just take whatever medicine the doctor gives me because I'm too old to run to the hills and look for the healing herbs.

Most younger people today can't even imagine what life was like or what this part of the country looked like during the first part of this century and some of them will just grin and shake their heads when I tell them all this stuff. But I'm going to tell you what it was like for me and every word's as true as the Gospel. So bear with me.

*Cliffie's grandparents,
Emily Munsey Bowles
and Anderson Bowles*

Chapter 2

The Origins of the Christian Appalachian Project – Helping People Help Themselves

Cliffie Strong would have been of immeasurable assistance to Father Ralph Beiting when he first envisioned the creation of an organization that would provide the human and financial resources necessary and specifically focused on helping Appalachian people lift themselves out of the bounds of poverty.

The Christian Appalachian Project learned, in its infancy and well before it was incorporated in 1964, that hooking up with the region's elder citizens and devouring their wisdom would be the best, if not only, way to figure out why our region seems to be so far behind the rest of the country in terms of educational achievement, economic development, human services and the host of other issues that make understanding poverty in Appalachia so complicated.

Father Ralph Beiting came to central Appalachia in the autumn of 1950. Assigned by Bishop William Mulloy, who then headed the Diocese of Covington, Father Beiting was charged with the responsibility of establishing a Catholic Mission in a mountainous, four-county area of rural eastern Kentucky that he fondly recalls as literally being the size of the state of Rhode Island. Ordained just a year earlier, he had been serving as Assistant Pastor in a Northern Kentucky parish and teaching math at highly regarded Newport Catholic High School, which, coincidentally, was his old Alma Mater. His parents and several siblings lived nearby.

Life was comfortable and good when he took the call from Bishop Mulloy. He had no idea why a first year assistant priest would be summoned to meet the Bishop and even after the meeting, he was perplexed because he didn't know whether or not he was being promoted or punished. But the orders were to pack his bags and head for Appalachia.

Father Beiting first arrived in Berea, Kentucky, took a look around and immediately discovered that living conditions were not what he was accustomed to in the Cincinnati suburbs. In the first place there was no Catholic Church—at least no rectory. That would have to be built. In the second place his new living quarters consisted of a house with a sagging roof and rotted floors and the Bishop had told him he needed to transform that into both living space and a Chapel until he and the congregation could build a proper Church. The congregation then consisted of six adults and three children.

Father Beiting came to Berea with a simple charge. Establish the Church and lead it. But as he looked out on the outlying counties he came to realize many families' physical needs were at least as great as their spiritual needs and thus began a ministry that catered to both. The farther he ventured off the main road, the more he found living conditions not significantly different from those that Cliffie will describe throughout her story.

But unlike the times in Cliffie's youth, when poverty was taken for granted, if it was recognized at all, he found despair and hopelessness. He found children malnourished and inadequately clothed because the mountain homesteads had been carved up into plots long ago worn out and now too small to farm or provide a living. He found homes falling apart and without indoor plumbing.

He found no jobs and countless adults educationally unprepared to cope with job requirements in mid-western cities. He found that young people who did manage to finish high school or complete some college or trade school caught the first bus out of Appalachia and headed north. He found countless elderly folks with no retirement benefits or health care living alone and dependent on what little cash their children might be able to send from Detroit, Indianapolis, Chicago, Dayton, Columbus or name your favorite industrial mid-western city.

With the help of his family, the old house in Berea was promptly made durable and before too long a Church was built. In the meantime he had discovered that hundreds of families had physical needs as great as their spiritual needs. Father Beiting was making weekly and often daily trips to and from the Northern Kentucky area where he gathered up food, clothing and household goods that he could deliver to needy families.

One night as he was nearing Berea after a long and tiring day, Father Beiting pulled off the side of the road to rest a minute while pondering his situation. At that moment he decided that he could not accomplish much in the way of a ministry if he was simply going to be a truck driver. And so commenced the vision that would eventually lead to the formation of the Christian Appalachian Project. Father Beiting realized that poverty was such an overwhelming problem that one man could not make a dent in it. If it were going to be solved, the people would have to do it themselves.

As the old Proverb goes, "Give someone a fish and you've fed him for a day. Teach someone to fish, you've fed him for a lifetime."

Father Beiting decided then and there, that if he were to have any success in Appalachia, he would have to teach folks to fish for themselves.

Chapter 3

Cliffie's Story continues (living off the land)

We always went to bed at dark and woke up way before daylight and as soon as we had breakfast, we went to work. You learned to walk fast and stay out of the way. By the time you were five years old or so, you could do something to help out even if was finding the hens' nests and gathering the eggs. You could help wash dishes or you could pack water for them that did. You could pack in kindling to build a fire the next morning. If you were old enough and there was something that needed doing somebody would put you at it.

I used to get up, way before daylight, and go to the barn to milk the cows in wintertime. I'd be so cold and sleepy that I'd milk awhile and then I'd lay down right there in the corner of the old cow's stall in the warm spot where she'd been bedded down. I'd doze off and take me a little nap because she was warm and the weather was so cold it made you hurt all over. She'd stand right there and let me take my little nap while she ate some fodder or a few ears of corn. Then I'd wake back up after a few minutes and go back to milking.

You can't find a good, gentle, Jersey or Gurnsey cow anymore like the ones we had, that will give two gallons of milk every milking. And you sure can't find anybody who would get their children out of bed at daylight and make them go to the barn and do the milking by hand now. But I did for over sixty years, and it is one of the most precious memories of my life. Carrying that good warm milk from the barn and back to the house when I was just a child still makes me feel warm all over. If I had a good milking cow right now, I'd be right there with her every morning and every night. I'd have to give the milk away because I don't need much but people don't know what they are missing out on if they have never had warm milk straight from the cow.

Most of my Dad's land was steep hillside but we cut down the timber here and there and grubbed out roots to make little hillside fields to grow our corn and beans. The ground was rich but the work was hard. Big tree stumps would be standing and we had to cut off the sprouts to keep them from shading the crop. And of course the ground was rocky. Even before I was big enough to do any hoeing, I'd be out there in the spring before planting, rolling rocks out of the field so they wouldn't buck a plow. To this day I can't stand the sight of rocks in my garden if they are half as big as a hen egg.

And we had a little flat bottomland, down at the foot of the hill on the creek bank that was easy to tend and especially good for growing hay. We kept some livestock—hogs mostly or calves and lambs that we butchered, and we also had chickens, ducks, geese and turkeys for eggs and meat. We usually kept at least four milk cows so that two of them would be fresh (giving milk) while the other two were dry during their breeding cycles. We churned our own butter and I have always liked buttermilk better than whole milk. We kept milk and butter and sometime meat cooled in a spring or in a bucket down in the well during hot weather but mostly we ate it up about as fast as it came in.

We worked awful hard to keep ourselves going but we rarely needed much hard money. You could always swap garden stuff or eggs and milk for what you needed out of the store, and that was mostly flour, salt, baking soda and sometimes sugar. But mostly we sweetened with molasses.

My Dad had a gristmill that was powered by a 42 horsepower engine that ran on kerosene so people would come from miles and miles around on grinding day to have their corn ground into meal. People paid him by giving him a turn (about a gallon) of shelled corn out of every bushel he ground for them. So we always had plenty cornbread on the table. We had meal to swap for stuff we didn't have. People today don't know what they're missing. Store bought meal is more like flour today and it sure doesn't taste like corn.

We brine-pickled a bunch of different vegetables such as corn, beans, cabbage for sour kraut, cucumbers, beets, and so forth. We used big five to fifteen gallon crocks or we put stuff up in quart or half gallon jars and kept them in a smoke house or a root cellar. We had that to eat all winter even if it was about the same thing every day. The brine, made of salt and water generally kept stuff from freezing too hard and preserved it at the same time.

In cold weather we would kills hogs and cure the meat out so it would keep for a few months. We'd make sausage and can it so we could have meat in warm weather. We also ground up a lot of beef, fried it good and done, drained it, salted it a little, and packed it away in crocks that we sealed with tallow and that's how we kept beef to eat in warm weather.

My Dad could eat hash three meals a day. You made it by taking ground beef you had put up and mixing it about half and half with diced up potatoes and onions and a little salt and pepper and maybe a little sage. It was hard to keep beef any other way because you can't salt it down or smoke it the way you can pork and still have it fit to eat. Salt will wash right out of pork but when it's in beef, it's there to stay.

We dried a lot of stuff, especially beans, apples, peaches, black-eyed peas, pumpkins and cushaws and so forth. We grew onions that would keep all winter, and of course, we always raised and holed up many bushels of potatoes.

Potatoes were holed by digging a deep, circular hole in the ground; maybe four feet deep and six feet across. The bottom of the hole and the sides were lined with straw or dry corn stalks to soak up any moisture.

Then you put several bushels of potatoes in and covered them with more straw or fodder and then a layer of leaves or whatever else you could find to keep rain or melting snow from soaking into the hole. Cover the whole thing with a foot or so of dirt and your potatoes would keep all winter and you had them to eat the next spring before the garden crops started coming in.

You could also turn a cabbage head, leaves and all, upside down and bury it in the ground with the root stuck up and it would keep fresh way up into cold weather.

We also harvested a lot of stuff that grew wild. There was all kinds of greens such as plantain, poke, creeses (which is what we called water cress) wild mustard and so forth. We packed in chestnuts, walnuts and hickory nuts by the bushel sack loads. Chestnuts were my favorite because they were easy to hull out. You could boil or bake them or eat them raw and just one of them made a mouthful.

Of course the blight had killed off all the chestnut trees by the time I was a grown woman so people cut most of them down after they died out for lumber and to make fence posts and split rail fences. Chestnut was probably the best timber in the woods. It was hard as rock and it would keep forever. I'm sure there are some old Chestnut fence posts and rail fences still standing if a person looked for them.

We kept fish traps in Big Sturgeon Creek and we had fish for supper anytime there was a high tide. Fish would come up out of the river and swim up Big Sturgeon Creek and the trap would catch them when they went out. We also killed a lot of game, especially rabbits and squirrels, during warm weather when hog meat or beef wouldn't cure or we had just plain run out of anything to butcher.

We had to eat lean a few times in the winter, but we never really got on the verge of bad starvation that I can remember because it seemed like somebody else was always worse off than we were no matter how bad our guts may have been growling. We sometimes did without a lot of stuff that other people took for granted, such as brought on shoes and clothes or anything else that came from a store. But we got by and actually, if we all made it through the winter and came out alive, we thought we were pretty well off compared to a lot of others. They blamed it on this disease or that but the truth is that a lot of people died of sickness they wouldn't have got in the first place if they'd had enough to eat. Many a death was blamed on consumption but if you laid the blame where it ought to be, it was plain old starvation at the root.

But we little children would pull tricks when I was young that would make the hair stand right up on the back of your neck if you knew that one of your youngens was doing something so stupid in this day and age.

One time me and my brother; I must have been about 10 and he was about 8; were sitting around and it had been raining all day and all of the night before and we decided we would go check that fish trap that Dad kept in the creek. So we got down to the creek and I pulled up the legs of my bloomers, which came down way below my knees. I rolled them up as high as I could. The legs were much bigger around than pants that a lot of people wear now. Then I pulled up my dress tail and tucked the hem into the waistband of my bloomers and I was ready to wade right out into that creek.

I would not have done that in front of anybody else but my brother and it didn't bother either one of us a bit. We were very young at the time and we used the same water, one right after another, when we had a chance to take a tub bath in cold weather. And during the summer time we scrubbed off in the creek anyway.

My brother rolled his pant legs up, he had on overalls, as far as they would go up his legs and rolled and tucked them in as high as they would go and then right out into that creek we waded even though the water was high and getting higher every minute, but we wanted to see if there was any fish in that trap because fish made a really special meal back then.

Well, the water current got us and washed us around but somehow we hung onto each other and got back to the bank and I was still alive and still had my bloomers on. We never realized that we were staring death in the eyes. We could have been drowned right then and there and probably should have been washed away. But God was watching over us and He rescued us from that flooded creek. We didn't even know it at the time, but I know it now.

And to this day I don't remember whether or not there was a fish in that trap when we finally did check on it. On the other hand, I don't remember being scared then, but it would have worried me to death if my own children had pulled a trick like that and I knew about it. We could have been drowned in a heartbeat or the twinkling of an eye but God was watching over us.

I believe firmly that God is always watching over us even when we put ourselves in peril. If life was a chance, half the children on earth would never live to be grown. If God is not looking over our children then He must have angels who do because you know as well as I do that we can't keep our eyes on them every minute.

Chapter 4

Without Volunteers There would be no CAP

As a child, Cliffie would have loved CAP's first big undertaking. She would also have been amazed by the volunteers, from other parts of the country, who came to Appalachia to help realize the CAP vision. And they would have been just as amazed by her.

In 1957, with the help of dozens of volunteers, Cliffview Lodge, a camp for children, complete with lodging and modern conveniences, was constructed and staffed by caring people who worked without compensation. It sat on a large cliff overlooking a large central Kentucky lake. Volunteers spent summers or even whole years of their lives helping to build hope and ambition among mountain children and keep the camp thriving.

When CAP was incorporated in 1964, it consisted of dozens of volunteers, enlisted locally and from midwestern Catholic Parishes, who were energetic, spiritually driven and able and willing to assist in tackling the myriad of problems that Appalachian families faced as a result of impoverishment.

They came singly, as married couples and as family units. They came in groups, by the van or busloads, to help repair homes that were frequently unfit for human habitation. They brought food, clothing and medical supplies and distributed them to families on the verge of starvation. They brought professional skills in carpentry, nursing, teaching, counseling and a host of other disciplines.

But more importantly, they brought love and the spiritual motivation to give a portion of their lives in service to their less-fortunate brothers and sisters in whatever capacity met the greatest need. Some could only stay a week or two. Others gave a season or so. Hundreds committed to a year or more and a few wound up serving for more than a decade.

Without those thousands of volunteers in the first decade of its existence, there would be no Christian Appalachian Project. And today, without the several hundred volunteers who discover CAP and enlist in volunteer service year in and year out, its program services would be severely diminished.

Today, volunteers from all over the nation and often from other countries, choose central Appalachia, specifically eastern Kentucky, as the destination for fulfillment of their spiritual desire to be of service to mankind.

Vast improvements have, in fact, been made throughout the region in physical infrastructure development such as roads, public water lines, schools, health care facilities, public housing, etc. since the sixties.

Unfortunately, more than 100,000 families in CAP's service area still live in abject poverty. Thousands of families still live in homes so deteriorated that they barely turn the elements. They are not insulated and the roofs leak. They are unsafe because they are improperly wired and ventilated. Frequently they catch fire and burn to the ground.

Replacing a home or making it safe is a fairly easy thing to do. It takes hard work, for sure, but the real building is more spiritual in nature and involves working with thousands of Appalachian children and adults who need a bit of love and guidance to help them figure out what they might be able to accomplish and make of their lives. That's where CAP really needs volunteers. It's easy enough to drive a nail into a shingle or a piece of wood. It's much more difficult to hammer encouragement and ambition into the human spirit.

Today CAP has numerous volunteer "houses" also called communities, scattered throughout its eastern Kentucky service area which covers more than 4,000 square miles in eastern Kentucky. Besides providing comfortable havens for folks in voluntary service, they serve as communal and spiritual enclaves for volunteers. On average, more than 50 volunteers are committed to voluntary service with CAP at any given time.

In addition to long-term volunteers, hundreds of college students show up every spring to help repair homes. Hundreds of others join church groups to come and spend a week or so helping out wherever they are needed. Dozens more spend their summers as counselors in CAP summer camps. The most common comment you will hear from a volunteer upon departing Appalachia may surprise you.

"The people of Appalachia that I served gave back to me more than I gave them."

Chapter 5

Cliffie's Story continues (growing up and going to school)

In my youth the only way to get around was to walk. The grownups, mostly the men, had horses or mules to ride but not the young people, unless they were boys nearly grown. Owning a riding horse back then would be about the same as owning a car in this day and time. So when we went visiting we walked from place to place, sometimes several miles in one direction.

Any time we had company at our place and they got ready to leave, we would always tell them that we wished they didn't have to leave and if it was getting late we would try to get them to stay all night. But when they did start to leave we'd always say, "Wait a minute and we'll walk a piece with you," and we'd walk part of the way home with them. And when we did part company, the last thing we would do is tell them to be sure and come back soon and they would always tell us to come and see them as soon as we could. That was just a common courtesy and everybody did it.

You never passed a person's house without them inviting you to come in and visit for a spell. Sometimes you would stop in if you needed a drink of water. If it was dinnertime or supper, most people would be right insulted if you didn't come in and take a meal with them. It didn't matter if all you had was cornbread and water gravy, you were always happy and proud to share whatever you had with your neighbors at mealtime and you never begrudged a bite to a visitor, neighbor or stranger, no matter how sparse the meal might be.

When you were in a hurry and didn't have time to stop, you'd holler howdy to each other and always invite folks to go home with you even though you didn't have time to visit them.

Annual school sessions were short and only lasted for six months or less. School started in late July and lasted through cold weather. But I usually could not go the first month or two because we had crops to get in. But when the weather got too bad to work in the fields we went to school. I went several years to Hickory Flat School, which was about a mile from our house. I don't remember when I started but I must have been 8 or 9 years old. I know I finished when I was 17 years old and

I had learned all that school could teach me. There was no road to the school to speak of. In dry weather people used the creek bed to get sleds or wagons in and out, but mostly when we were walking, we followed a little crooked path that ran around the side of the hill.

As I said before, we only got just one pair of shoes a year and that was just for cold weather. We girls got the same, plain old leather work shoes as the boys. With all the walking we had to do, we never wore shoes unless the ground was froze or if it was so cold you had to have something on your feet to keep from getting frostbite. Many a time I've carried my shoes to save wear and tear but even then they'd be completely worn out by early spring.

Anyway, we had a neighbor about halfway between our place and Hickory Flat who kept a big hog lot right beside the path. Many a time I've climbed across the fence of that hog lot on my way to or from school and made an old sow get up and I would stand in the bed where she'd been laying so I could warm my feet.

The school was actually an old log building, just one room and one teacher for all eight grades and it pretty much taught itself. We only had forty or fifty pupils at the most at any given time. The teacher spent a lot of time on the more advanced children and then they helped the younger ones so you learned a lot by doing.

We didn't have many books to speak of and shared what we did have. I only had two books that I could actually call my own the whole time I was in school. The school had a set or two of reading, spelling and arithmetic books with different levels depending on how advanced you were. So we would sit together and share the same book to do whatever lesson we were working on.

We were not tested. I never once took a written test the whole time I was in school. The students were at such different levels of learning that it would not have made sense. We proved what we had learned by reciting and showing that we knew our multiplication tables and such. But let me tell you, back then you didn't need a lot of schooling. Learning to survive would teach you a lot more than you could ever learn in a schoolroom. At least it would teach you more of the practical lessons you had to know to get by in life.

But I learned to read and make sense of the Bible and about anything else I picked up. I learned how to write well enough to send a sensible letter. I learned all the basic arithmetic I needed to manage what little money came my way and take care of any counting and measuring I had to do. I never saw a dictionary or realized there was such a thing until long after I had finished school.

I was eleven years old before I ever saw a gravel road. We were on our way to a ball game in Lee County and all of a sudden we came up on a road that was covered with white limestone gravel. I didn't even know there was such a thing but it was all so smooth and no mud holes in it.

I was a grown woman before I ever went to McKee, the county seat of Jackson County about 12 miles from home. My third child was a baby before I ever went to Booneville, the County seat of Owsley County so that would have been 1939 and I would have been 24 years old.

I've only been out of the state three or four times and one of those was when I went to see about my son who was hurt bad while he was in the Air Force. My youngest boy and I rode the bus to Miami, Florida so we could go see about him. I went to Indiana one time to visit some kinfolks and I've been to Texas to visit my youngest daughter.

I remember well the first car I ever saw. It was after dark and we saw these big bright lights coming up the holler side by side and you could hear the motor puttering along. I heard about automobiles before but I had never seen one. It was my

Aunt and Uncle coming in to visit. It must have been some sort of Holiday. I don't remember for sure but I know some of my schoolmates also had company come in driving cars and the next day at school we were all talking about chopping wood after dark by the lights of those cars. That's how bright they were.

One evening we were walking a piece down the road with my cousins who had come to visit and we heard this loud noise in the sky. It was an airplane, the first one I'd ever seen and we thought that was something. It was something we'd heard talk of but you don't know whether to believe it or not until you actually lay eyes on one. For some reason 1924 sticks in my mind so I must have been about nine years old.

As I will tell you more about later, I've always been pretty enterprising. When I've needed a dollar or two, I've generally been able to figure out a way to earn it. I also learned at an early age that even the best of business ideas can get you in trouble if you don't use some common sense.

One time when I was a young girl, I ordered a big box of gum that I was going to sell on consignment to the other kids in school. I thought I'd be able to make enough profit on it to buy some brought on toys like maybe a rubber ball or some balloons or maybe some ribbons or hair bows. There's any number of things a young girl wanted back then that she couldn't get if she didn't have a little money. Let's just say that I had plans for my profit before I sold a stick of gum.

Oh goodness! That gum smelled so good but it was not selling as fast as I thought it would and before long my sister and I had chewed most of it ourselves. Well the people who had let me have the gum wanted their money and I didn't have anything to pay them with except for empty wrappers and I knew that was not going to fly. So I wound up having to go into the woods and dig May Apple root to raise enough money to pay for it. I would have been a lot better off if I had just dug May Apple in the first place and never seen that gum. But it taught me a lesson about good intentions. You can intend all day long but nothing is going to happen until you get up and go to work and make it happen.

During recess at school we played marbles, tag or whatnot. I was always a tomboy and generally was not interested in stuff that most of the girls took up. I always had a couple of pocketknives to whittle or carve with or play mumbely peg, which was a simple and safe little tossing game. Of course you also had to have a knife to make whistles and carve little doodads which I've done all my life. And of course I learned to sew and cook out of necessity because we had to make and mend most of the clothes we wore.

I know that knives are only fit to cause trouble in the schools anymore. So before you go to raising your eyebrows, let me explain that a little pocketknife was almost necessary for survival when I was young.

They were never, ever used for violence or considered weapons by any stretch of the imagination. But you needed one to cut a little sprout and sharpen it so you could roast a little piece of meat or a slice of potato. Or skin a squirrel or rabbit.

You could slice off a piece of bark from a cinnamon bush or a hickory limb and use it to tie about anything including a broken shoestring. You could peel an apple or a peach or whatever needed peeling. You could whittle out whistles or toys, trim your finger or toenails or dig the dirt out from under them.

You could cut the tops off onions or carrots when you went to the garden or use them to harvest anything that had a stalk. You could cut short pieces of leather to mend a harness or a strip of bark to mend a chair bottom. You could even trim your hair if you had a mind to. They had short little blades of just two or three inches and the blades folded back into the handle, so they were not dangerous at all to carry. And if you did get cut with one, it was because you accidentally cut yourself.

I could beat most of the boys at about anything. We traded knives all the time and I can't ever remember not getting the best part of a pocketknife trade. And all my life I've always had a good pocketknife or two but I don't keep them just to look at. A good pocketknife is about the handiest thing anybody can have if they know how to use one and how to keep it sharp enough to whittle with.

People would have thought you were awful bad off if you were so poor you couldn't afford a pocketknife when I was growing up. Even today, I couldn't get along without one and I sure don't carry it with any intention of hurting somebody with it. But when you are out in the garden and the tomatoes and cucumbers are ripe and you want to peel or slice something to eat right off the vine, I don't see how you can get along without a little knife in your pocket.

Cliffie with a few of her creations...

...and carving a wooden chain

Chapter 6

Youth and Children

From the very beginning, CAP recognized that Appalachia's future lay in its younger generation. Children, from preschoolers to teenagers, needed to be nurtured and encouraged. They needed spiritual development and they needed to learn to be responsible for themselves and their behavior.

For decades, CAP has run early childhood development centers, strategically situated to serve children in especially distressed communities. In a nutshell, CAP believes that the attitudes and ambition children develop in their early years will influence them for the rest of their lives. Parents are also involved in the centers so that they can learn educational techniques used by the teachers and also how to provide gentle discipline for inappropriate behavior.

All of CAP's youth programs, from early childhood development centers to summer camps have a strong focus on nutrition. Children are provided healthy, nutritious meals and encouraged to eat well at regular mealtimes. Kids discover that nutritious foods, fruits and vegetables especially, taste better than sugar-filled and fatty junk foods and that they feel better and have more energy when they eat properly. They take those lessons home and parents discover that good food is less expensive than junk.

Several CAP child development centers have achieved national certification and many of the center managers have become leaders in developing state policy as it relates to early childhood development.

CAP has also, for decades, run youth and teen centers to provide both recreational and educational opportunities for the region's most at-risk children.

CAP youth workers offer tutoring in difficult academic subjects. The youth and teen centers foster responsibility by organizing community service projects that may be as simple as mowing an elderly person's lawn to cleaning up discarded refuse along miles of public highway. The centers are largely staffed by young, Christian volunteers who serve as appropriate role models. Teenagers, especially, frequently form bonds with volunteers that will last a lifetime.

CAP also provides weeklong summer camping experiences and off-season retreats for more than a thousand young people each year.

None of these youth would have the opportunity to experience a well-structured summer camping experience. CAP camps provide a multitude of organized activities, learning experiences and spiritual development. Dozens of volunteer counselors from all over the country spend several weeks of their summer vacations staffing these facilities during the camping seasons. Professional nurses provide health screening to campers and serve on the camps' staff full time during the summer sessions. Full-time program managers and volunteers assure that the camps have year-round activities for both adults and youth as other CAP programs may need them.

Remotely located deep in the heart of the mountains, CAP camps have secure dormitory style lodging facilities. Nutritious meals are served in cafeterias. Campers have work assignments every day that range from washing dishes, cleaning rest rooms, mopping floors and numerous other chores necessary to keep the facilities clean and tidy. They may also be involved in camp improvement projects such as building new hiking trails, planting flowerbeds or applying a coat of paint when it is needed.

The camps have waterfronts for canoeing and fishing as well as modern swimming pools, crafts facilities, and miles of hiking trails through the forest. Campers meet their peers from many other communities and they go home with an experience they will remember for the rest of their lives. They also go home with a sense of pride and prestige because they have had an experience that may have cost their more affluent peers several hundred dollars.

The camps, as well as the teen centers, provide leadership development programs that help participants develop and shape appropriate values that will not only enhance their personal development, but also make them responsible leaders for the region's future.

Chapter 7

Cliffie's Story continues
(coming of age & getting married)

So yes, I was a tomboy but I think it served me well. By the time I was grown I could work as hard as most men, but I never took any interest in boys from a romance point of view until after I turned seventeen. I'd never had a date or gone walking or even held hands with a boy and I didn't have any interest in them. I'd never been struck on one.

I had always dreamed of getting a college education and traveling to far away places and seeing what the world was like outside the hills of old Kentucky. Those plans and dreams didn't have room for any man, or least for any I knew much about at the time. I figured I'd find the right man somewhere down the road after I'd had a chance to see more than the ones who lived there in our little part of Jackson County.

Of course that goes right back to those good intentions I spoke of earlier. There wasn't any way for a girl my age to get out of the hills. It was going to take way more money than I knew how to get my hands on.

I worked hard, but I bought my own clothes with what little money I could get from selling berries and herb roots such as May Apple, ginseng and yellow root (also known as golden seal). My Daddy let my brother and me clear out a laurel thicket down near the creek to grow us a little patch of tobacco. The money we made off that was our clothing allowance but every nickel I could scrape up was needed for something else.

I do remember buying a pair of tennis shoes once with my tobacco money and they looked so much prettier than the old work shoes that I'd always had. Anyway, a day or two after I got them, I was walking down the road and slipped and got one of them stuck in a mud hole. I ran back to the house and washed the mud out as best I could and stuck it in the oven to dry. But it never looked like much after that.

But what really killed my dreams and ambitions was the Great Depression, which was in full swing in my seventeenth year. Nobody had any money so you couldn't sell a thing or hardly make a dime. If Dad hadn't owned his farm I don't know what we would have done. But at least we could grow enough to eat on. Many times I would get up way before daylight and walk ten miles on cold frosty mornings to strip tobacco for 50 cents a day and then walk back home that night. I'd eat a little bite, sleep awhile and then head back out the next morning. By the time I got to the barn, the front of my coat would be solid ice where my breath had froze on it.

Under normal circumstance I should have been paid at least 50 cents an hour. A lot of younger people don't believe that and the ones that do, ask me why on earth I did it. Well, I will tell you, if I hadn't been a good work hand and mighty fast at stripping tobacco there wouldn't have been any paying work for me at all and even that only lasted for a few weeks.

Sometimes we would get some grubbing work, digging out stumps and clearing new ground, the hardest back breaking work you can think of and the pay was still 50 cents a day. It took over a week's pay to buy a pair of shoes.

"Root old hog, or die," is an old saying in the mountains meaning that if you don't get out there and find something to eat yourself, nobody else is going to do it for you and you're going to starve to death. There's never been a worse time in this country for a young person to enter adulthood

Portrait of the Strong family, including Cliffie's husband, Vernon (standing, fourth from left)

than the Great Depression except for maybe war times. But there has never been a day since that I didn't feel blessed and thankful for what little I may have had.

The first time I saw my future husband, he had come to our house to take my mother to catch the train to Heidelburg in Lee County. After that he started trying to spark with my older sisters, but the only thing he gave me was just teasing and aggravating. I gave him as good as he got.

After I got a little older, about the time I turned 17, he gave up getting any of my sisters so him and me started taking walks together and before long were holding hands and I guess I let him kiss me a time or two.

So one thing led to another and pretty soon we discovered that we had a lot in common when it boiled right down to bare facts. We had stopped teasing each other and I guess you could say that the love bug was biting both of us on the heels. We were really happy when saw each other and not so cheerful when we were apart. It got to be plain as the nose on your face that we were meant for each other.

I turned 18 in October and we got married on the fourth day of April in 1934. Vernon had to borrow the money for us to get married on. He was trying to keep his parents' old farm going and owed some money he had borrowed to keep it up, but we plunged right in. If we had waited until he got out of debt, we'd have been waiting for the rest of our lives.

I told him all his life that he tried to marry every sister I had but I was the only one smart enough to take him. He'd just grin and not say anything because he knew I was right.

Vernon and Cliffie in her new dress. Cliffie swept the local school for a year to earn enough money to make her dress.

Chapter 8

Adult Education

Cliffie dreamed of a better life, of getting an education and traveling. But reality for her was not unlike the circumstances that exist for many Appalachian adults today. Certainly there are more opportunities for young people than existed in Cliffie's time but all too often their dreams have not been realized.

Unfortunately, huge numbers of Appalachian adults made decisions in their youth that sentenced them to lives of poverty even though they didn't know it at the time. The tendency to marry too young has rapidly declined over the last decade and CAP's teen programs, as previously discussed, can take some credit for that. The high school dropout rate has dropped dramatically and a greater percentage of young people are coming to realize that they have no future without an education. Still, thousands of adults are unprepared for college or trade school. Many can't read beyond a first or second grade level or even complete a job application.

Thousands and thousands of Appalachia's current adult population never finished high school and a likewise number never even started. Their chances of finding a job or getting a promotion that pays a livable wage are practically non-existent.

CAP Adult Education Centers offer both classroom and one-on-one instruction that includes everything from basic literacy to state-certified, high school equivalency (GED) diplomas to preparation for college entrance exams and even tutoring for adults enrolled in college classes.

CAP has also established classrooms in remote communities, utilizing country church basements or community centers where space was available and offers classes to adults who have no transportation or find it impractical to drive relatively long distances to town. These classrooms, too, are equipped with computers, up-to-date instructional material and staffed by professional teachers.

Both salaried and volunteer teachers work one-on-one with twenty-five to fifty adults at a time to help students improve their education levels and become more prepared to find employment in our ever-changing world. Teachers meet adult students where they are in terms of educational achievement and then help them move forward.

The nuts and bolts of CAP's Adult Education Program has traditionally focused on completing a GED curriculum and passing a state administered test certifying that students have passed the academic requirements for a high school equivalence diploma.

Several hundred adults have reached that milestone by utilizing CAP's Adult Education Program. Many have gone on to complete college degrees and all either have or at least they are better prepared to participate in the work force.

CAP arranges graduation exercises for students who complete the program, complete with traditional cap and gown and diplomas presented by the local school superintendent. The sense of pride and accomplishment is so intense at these ceremonies that frequently there is not a dry eye in the house.

Educational development and technical training are such wonderful and rewarding paths to follow for adults who want to escape the bounds of poverty. However, resources to provide them are few and far between in the mountains.

In addition to the straightforward academic preparation CAP has, for several years, run readiness training through its Adult Education

Program. Even with a high school or GED diploma, many adults lack the confidence to approach employers and interview for a job. Lack of self-esteem is often the greatest obstacle. Oftentimes participants have been too modest to detail their skills and qualifications on a resume because it sounds like boasting.

CAP has enabled hundreds of adult education participants to get a real sense of what it is like in a workplace, helped them develop conflict resolution skills, helped them develop a sense of courage and ultimately helped a large percentage of them find permanent employment.

CAP realizes that quality employers are not going to locate in Appalachia unless and until the region demonstrates a higher commitment to educational development. CAP's Adult Education endeavors not only demonstrate that commitment but also prove it by the sheer number of potential adult employees who have chosen to further their educational qualifications.

Chapter 9

Cliffie's Story continues (starting a family)

We moved to Owsley County, which was not that far away from where I grew up, and for the most part we have lived here ever since. For the first ten years we rented a few different places but we also farmed some on his family's land and some on my Dad's place and we hired out to work for other people too. Wages were still pitiful and the Depression had not let up a bit that I could tell. I was still just making fifty cents a day when we were first married but Vernon had a pair of mules and he could make a little more.

Vernon was a real muleskinner. He was a hard-working man but he was gentle and patient, which you have to be if you are going to get much work out of a mule before it drives you crazy. Vernon's mules loved him as much as he loved them and he could get work out of them that the best-trained horse in the world couldn't accomplish. He would make them walk backwards to tilt heavy posts up so they would fit in the holes. He could take a pair of mules and outwork a tractor and he could work and tend ground so steep that a tractor would not have stood upright on it if you could have got one there to begin with.

But I never took a penny off of him for anything I needed. We had it worked out as to what he was responsible for and what I was responsible for and we got along just fine with that arrangement. I would say our marriage was better than most. I took care of my money and he took care of his and we were equal partners in our marriage. You might say I was a liberated woman long before they invented that term. I was way ahead of my time.

We lived here in Owsley County except for about nine months when we decided to move to Pulaski County, which was about seventy miles away. That was in 1941. We had heard talk about how much better the farmland was there and how much more prosperous it was and all that. But we didn't much care for it and the owner of the farm we were working wanted everything so we packed up and moved back to Owsely County and we stayed here ever since.

We had four children. They were all born at home. Edith, the oldest one was born on the last day of December, 1934. Vernon went to get the

Cliffie surrounded by her four children, (from left) Edith, James Lloyd, Lucille, and Jesse Darrell

doctor but Edith got there way before Vernon got back with him. She lives in Lexington now. Edith was born on a Monday and the day before, I had ridden a horse five miles each way to go visit my mother.

James Lloyd was born in 1936 on the first day of November. Vernon went to get my mother who was a midwife and James Lloyd almost beat her there, too. James Lloyd just lives around the ridge here but he is badly disabled from brain damage he suffered from an accident while he was in the Air Force.

Lucille was born in 1939 on the seventeenth day of January. She was there thirty minutes after my

Cliffie's daughter, Etta Lucille Lamb, Chief Warrant Officer 3, US Army

water broke so there wasn't time to go get anybody until she was already there. Her home is in Texas but she has been staying with me since she retired from the Army and she is going to move back home this summer and be close to me. Lucille is the only one who finished high school and she also graduated from Berea College.

After her children were grown and her first husband died of lung cancer, she joined the Army when she was 42 years old. Lucille is a retired Chief Warrant Officer now after a wonderful 20-year career serving her country. Can you imagine joining the Armed Forces when you're old enough to be a grandma?!

Jesse Darrell, my baby one, was born on the ninth day of February in 1941. He was an easy birth too. But he lives in Heaven now. He died in November of 2002 at the age of sixty-one. He was working in Texas at the time and staying with Lucille and she found him sitting on the couch, dead. I don't care how old you live to be, there is nothing in the world that will hurt a mother as bad as losing a child. Here's a little poem I wrote for him:

An Ode to Jesse Darrell, My Youngest Son
By Mother, Cliffie Strong,
Date 12-10-2003

February the ninth, 1941
God gave us this baby son

I took this baby to my breast
I vowed I would do my best

To teach him as best I could
I felt that this was motherhood

At the age of 61
God called home our baby son

God took him home so he could rest
This baby boy I took to my breast

I know someday I'll meet him there
When I climb that golden stair

There will be so much joy
When I meet again, our baby boy

Cliffie's sons, Jesse Darrell and James Lloyd (left to right)

We bought this old hillside farm in 1942 after all the children were born. It was an old homestead that had been divided up into several tracts and we wound up buying three tracts from three different heirs. The tracts were all side-by-side. We also got the old home place and we lived there until we built the home I live in now. The land was cheap because it was pretty much worn out already and it was all grown up so we had to grub and clear every bit of it almost like starting from scratch. Most people who farmed by then, had given up on the hillsides but that was all that Vernon and me had ever known.

We bought the first tract on a land contract in 1942. We borrowed the money from the bank for the other two. The whole thing, house and all, cost fifteen hundred dollars, which may not sound like a lot of money, but it put us in debt for years. We finally paid the place off with cash from the crops and whatever work we could find doing for somebody else. We grew a tobacco crop and raised a few head of cattle. Later on, I bought the first gasoline chain saw ever seen in these parts which saved a lot of time and also let us do some logging and sell a load of firewood now and then and we used that money to help pay the place off.

I took in laundry from other people and washed their clothes by hand on scrub boards. I packed water from the creek and heated it in a big black kettle over open fires outside. I scrubbed their clothes with homemade lye soap and dried them outside in the open air. It was hard work, but at least it was a little paying work.

I did a lot of sewing for other people and I learned to put in home permanents for women. I scoured the hills for blackberries, huckleberries, gooseberries, raspberries and peddled them out. I'd get up in the morning, fix breakfast, straighten the house up a little and then I'd grab two ten gallon buckets and hit the hills.

I'd pick berries until it got so dark I couldn't tell whether they were green or ripe. I shelled out black walnuts by the bushel and sold the kernels by the quart. I've set up all night with a rock in my lap to crack walnuts on until the roosters crowed the next morning.

To tell you the truth I've always loved being outside and especially in the woods and I would rather eat stuff that grows wild than cultivated food. I guess it's the Indian blood in me. My grandmothers on both sides were part Indian but I don't know what tribes they were from.

I always grew a much bigger garden than we needed and I sold stuff out of it, especially shuck beans which are beans that you dry with the hulls on them and cook about the same way you would pinto beans or navy beans. People around here though like them better than any other dried beans so I could sell every one I had to spare and actually make more on them than green beans.

We kept chickens and cows so I had milk and eggs to sell or trade out at the store. We skimped by as much as we could and still grew about everything we needed to eat just like the old days. We didn't buy anything unless we had to have it. I made most of our clothes. I could always get a bargain on material. I've taken old pants legs, turned them upside down, ripped the seams out and sewed them together and made skirts for my girls to wear to high school.

We never wasted anything. If it had a hole in it, I patched it. If it broke, I figured how to put it back together.

To this day I have the same attitude. Two of the best aluminum cookers I use right now have patches on the bottom where I've fixed holes that wore through on the stove burner. If something is too wore out for me to use you can just about bet your last nickel that nobody else is ever going to get any use out of it.

We didn't have electricity, but the first real indulgence I ever had in modern terms was a washing machine powered by a gasoline motor. If you've never bent over and scrubbed every piece of laundry on the place by hand on a wash board, you don't have any idea how wonderful it was to have a machine that could do all the hard work for you. And besides that, it saved time that you could put to other use.

The first form of outside entertainment I ever allowed myself was an old battery-operated radio, which we bought in the forties. We didn't play it much to keep the battery from running down. We would listen to the news for 5 minutes and turn it off. We knew exactly when certain shows were coming in at night. The Lone Ranger, The Green Hornet, and Amos and Andy came out of WJJD in Chicago. These usually lasted 15 minutes. We might tune in the Wayne Raney show from WCKY in Cincinnati for a few minutes at night, and of

Big Springs School House

course we never missed the Grand Ole Opry on WSM out of Nashville on Saturday night.

When the children were younger, we never had to worry about them much. The little one room grade school they all four attended was in hollering distance of the house and you could see it from the garden. It was called Big Springs School and it was built in 1906 according to people who lived here all their lives. It's still standing. It's on a tract of land that joins ours. The site was actually part of the old farm that we bought part of before the heirs divided it up.

Chapter 10

Economic Development: Attics and Operation Sharing

All four of Cliffie's children had to leave the mountains to find work and make livings. Her oldest son, James Lloyd is back at home only because he suffered severe injuries that left him permanently and totally disabled.

Cliffie's children were not alone in being faced with the prospects of leaving home or staying in the mountains and facing starvation. However, unlike Cliffie's kids, many young people were educationally unprepared and had no idea how to cope with living in a world outside the mountains.

Conditions are not totally unlike that today. Far too many young people are unprepared to leave and unable to find work at home because opportunity simply does not exist. So they find themselves stuck in the same old poverty cycle that seems to get worse from year to year without noticeable improvement in conditions.

Long gone are the days when folks could live off the land. Gone are the timber resources. Infrastructure—water, sewer, gas/electrical power, flat land, and other amenities for industrial development are woefully inadequate if they exist at all. Transportation routes involve two-lane mountainous roads that are dangerous enough for automobiles and laughable for heavy trucking.

With few exceptions eastern Kentucky Counties had lower populations in 2000 than they did fifty years ago according to the US Census Bureau. The trend still continues in many places. Between 1990 and 2000, Owsley County, where Cliffie still lives, had a net decline of 3.5% in population. The bottom line is that the best and brightest young people are still leaving home to find work. Those who can't are literally trapped and it is the very young and very old who suffer most.

Along with basic human development programs, CAP realized that unemployment was not caused by the people but because there were no jobs.

In the early sixties CAP started up and managed a Christmas Wreath manufacturing plant in Jackson County that provided seasonal employment so that about 100 folks had opportunities to work for a few weeks after the tobacco harvest and supplement their normal income. That plant was sold to private ownership. Ditto for a broom factory later sold to a local college. Dozens of little enterprises, too numerous to list, were started up and turned back over to local residents.

An all out effort was made to show farmers that they could broaden their economic base by commercially growing tomatoes, cucumbers, bell peppers and even Christmas trees instead of sticking just to tobacco and livestock farming.

Almost from its very beginning, CAP has operated so-called Attic Stores that sell good used clothing, small appliances and miscellaneous household goods for a pittance of their actual value. After hauling load after load of donated goods back to the mountains and giving them away, CAP soon realized that it was fostering dependence instead of responsibility. The reasoning, and accurately so, was that folks had a much keener appreciation for material goods if they had something invested in them.

In the case of fire or natural disaster, the Attics have historically provided free clothing and other goods, but customers able to pay a bit are routinely asked to do so.

Though it may take several years to get an Attic's revenue up to break-even, the goal is to get them established and then have a local non-profit take over the management. Now community owned, Attics are scattered throughout the region and provide easily affordable goods to thousands of families. As you will later discover, Cliffie first became acquainted with CAP when she was shopping in an Attic Store.

After local management is secured, CAP continues to supply them with tons of donated clothing and other goods.

With two strategically placed warehouses containing over 100,000 square feet of floor space, two 18 wheel tractor-trailers and several smaller trucks, CAP's Operation Sharing procures and distributes large donations to nonprofit organizations throughout Appalachia. More than 125 corporate donors provide trailer loads of educational material, tons of food, clothing, building materials, home and office furniture, medical supplies, toiletries, sanitation supplies and a long list of other goods.

The value of these donated goods runs as high as $50 million annually. Operation Sharing uses its trucks to both pick up donations all across the country and then redistributes them to churches, Christian Missions and nearly 1,500 other nonprofit organizations located in all 13 Appalachian States. Eastern Kentucky is the biggest beneficiary of Operation Sharing because it is the most impoverished.

Operation Sharing has recently started a new initiative called Operation Relief that is designed to provide rapid response to natural disasters, particularly flooding caused by deforestation, and has received high praise from both nonprofits and disaster victims alike, particularly in Kentucky and West Virginia. By stockpiling and warehousing a huge range of durable goods and nonperishable food, Operation Relief can be at the site of disasters with huge truckloads of relief items almost as soon as the disaster occurs.

CAP also humbly recognizes that it cannot come close to solving all the region's problems and that material goods alone are not sufficient to help many community-based groups stay functional. CAP partners with hundreds of service organizations and offers them cash support through its Human Development Grants Program.

CAP Human Development Grants are used by small nonprofit groups throughout the region for nearly every worthwhile purpose imaginable. Frequently they are used to purchase educational supplies and equipment, repair facilities, supplement utility costs and whatever else may be required to help struggling service groups survive and prosper.

Community-based groups serving the spiritual, educational and material needs of the poor are simply required to complete a short application. A simple review of each applicant is conducted to verify legitimacy before funds are awarded. However, CAP has such a long history in the region that it knows most of the worthwhile organizations and is always willing to share its resources with them.

Chapter 11

Cliffie's Story continues (empty nest and a worn out house)

By 1955, the kids were old enough to pretty much take care of themselves and had minds of their own. Edith was married and moved away. James Lloyd was in the Air Force. Lucille was getting ready to finish high school. Jesse Darrell was determined to drop out of high school and get a job.

I have four children, nineteen grandchildren, thirty-five great-grandchildren and twelve great great grandchildren. But most of them are scattered to the four winds. There are very few jobs around here and we don't have any economy to speak of. Young people can't live off the land and have anything anymore. If they are going to work they don't have any choice but to pack up and leave. I have only one son close to me and he is totally disabled. His son, my grandson, lives with him and helps take care of him.

My husband, Vernon, was over fifty years old and he took a notion to buy a '53 Chevrolet pick-up. There was getting to be so much automobile traffic on the roads that it was getting dangerous to drive a wagon with a pair of mules if you wanted to go anyplace on a main road. But the faster an automobile would run, the more in a hurry people got and they had no patience if they got behind a wagon and couldn't pass it.

Now we had never owned a motor vehicle of any kind. That truck was our first and last automobile. I tell people to this day that Vernon wore it out between the feed shed and the barn lot because he never was comfortable driving it anyplace else. Oh, he would go to the store and maybe to Booneville once in awhile but he would be a nervous wreck every time he got out on the road. I think I could have handled it okay but he never would let me touch the wheel. I never was afraid of anything much but let me put it this way, I never rode that truck with him driving unless I needed something awful bad.

We didn't get electricity until 1959. At first all we had was a couple of light bulbs. I wanted a refrigerator so bad. I couldn't think of anything that would be more wonderful.

Home where Cliffie and Vernon raised their four children

An electric stove never crossed my mind and to this day I would rather heat with wood and cook on a wood stove if I had one. Anyway, I went through tobacco fields and picked up trash tobacco leaves that had fallen off when they were cutting it and that's how I paid for my first electric appliance. Later on I bought an electric washing machine and a radio so I didn't have to worry about gasoline for the washer or a battery for the radio anymore.

By the sixties all the kids were gone, but Vernon and me were working hard as ever. I don't remember the year but I sold some calves that we had raised, and that was the first real money we'd ever had to put aside that we could call our own. We didn't owe any debts and every penny that I didn't absolutely have to have, I started putting back because I knew we were going to have to have a better place to live and that our place was way beyond repair.

I didn't slow down a bit. I gardened just as much as ever but I had a lot more to sell since the children were all gone and I was able for the first time to start saving a little money from that. I took to making quilts. I pieced quilt tops for other people, which I dearly love to do to this day. So I made a little money off that. Nowadays, I make quilts for my friends, relatives and grandchildren so they'll have something to remember me by.

Vernon sold a pair of mules for a good price and someone offered him a good price for two milk cows which we didn't need any longer so that went in the bank. I already had in the back of my mind what we were going to do with the money but we hadn't talked about it much. But it was plain as day that our old house was falling apart and beyond repair. Termites had eaten the foundation until it was about ready to fall apart. Holes were worn in the chimneys and we were in constant worry that it would catch on fire. The roof was leaking so bad that we had to have buckets in every room to catch the rain and the rafters were so rotted that it would have been dangerous to even think about putting

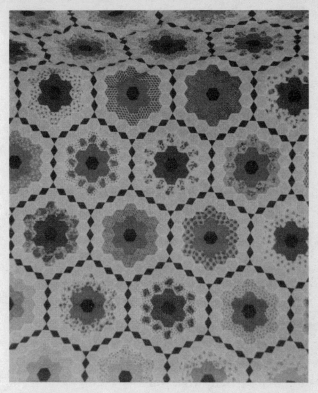

"Grandmother's Flower Garden" – Quilt top made by Cliffie

on a new roof. And it just kept getting worse and worse every year.

It got to the point that we feared for our lives if we had to live in it much longer.

One day I heard on the news or maybe I read it in the paper that money from the Farmer's Home

Administration was available to build homes for the elderly at 1% interest to upgrade their standard of living. They told what day the representative that took applications was going to be there in Booneville. So I got all my papers, my bank balance, proof that we owned our land and had it paid for, and our income statements together. I was over sixty at the time and Vernon was over seventy.

So I took my papers in and told the man I wanted to borrow enough money to build us a little house. He looked over my papers and he said, 'Ms. Strong there's a program that will give you an outright grant of $5,000 that you could use to repair the home you live in now.' I looked him straight in the eye and told him the termites had eaten most of the house, the roof was caving in and the chimneys were falling. I said, 'I don't know about you but I don't know anybody that has $5,000 to throw away and that's exactly what you'd be doing if you spent it on that house.'

He hum-hawed around and finally told me I couldn't get a loan because our income was too low. I told him I thought low income was what it was for.

Then he told me that our income was so low that we couldn't afford the payments and I said, 'That's what you think."

Now it was true that Vernon was only drawing thirty-seven dollars a month and I wasn't drawing anything and of course I had no way actually proving I earned a dime. But I told him I had been selling a little stuff and saving up to buy a house.

Then he wanted to know how much we had saved and I showed him my bank statements which showed that I'd been saving a little all along and that I still made a little off the farm and so forth. And I explained to him that prices were getting higher every day and we could not afford to pay eight or ten percent interest rates at the bank or to a house trailer outfit.

Not that I'd give you nickel for a trailer that might blow away in the first big wind and would be rusting down before you got it set up.

He just stood there and looked at me for a few seconds. Then he told me that people with steady jobs were in there every day and most of them couldn't make a nickel down payment. I showed him that we could.

He looked me straight in the eye and told me he'd see to it that I'd get the loan. A little bit after that we got the mortgage for 30 years at 1% interest.

We started on the house in November of 1978, and moved into it in April of 1979. Vernon died in

1988 and I paid the house off in 1995, seventeen years after we took out the loan. It's all free and clear now. It didn't cost much to build but I figure it's worth more now than what I paid to build it. It's good and warm and it don't leak. I'm lucky and I guess I'm a lot better off than some. But I can tell you this much, I worked out every penny it took to build this place.

Chapter 12

Christian Appalachian Project Housing Program

Cliffie's and Vernon's home was beyond repair but fortunately she was able to come up with the financing to build a new one. Most Appalachian families who live in dangerous housing are not so fortunate.

Substandard housing is an overwhelming problem in Appalachia. Thousands of families live in homes that are literally unsafe for human habitation. They are often so drafty and leaking so badly that they scarcely turn the elements. They are improperly wired and ventilated. Every winter hundreds of families in CAP's service area lose their homes and all their belongings to fire. Some even lose their lives.

While the current emphasis of CAP's Housing Program is focused on emergency repair, it has frequently built modest, safe, dry, dwellings for elderly people so that they would have physical comfort in their waning years. CAP also provides emergency shelter for burn out victims and assists them in finding suitable housing until they can get back on their feet. The Housing Program also provides emergency repairs and renovation on an ongoing basis. Several paid staff and numerous volunteers work year round in the program. Frequently church groups or other volunteers will come on a short-term basis and make major repairs for families in desperate situations.

CAP has found a way to make a significant dent in the housing problem. Every year the Housing Program joins forces with CAP's Volunteer Program to organize an initiative called WorkFest.

Several hundred college students, from dozens of campuses across the country, converge on Appalachia and spend their spring breaks repairing homes for needy families. They replace roofs, siding, windows and doors. They install insulation, replace unsafe flues and stove pipes, build steps and porches and even build room additions on homes that are overcrowded.

WorkFest volunteers not only work long hours all week when they arrive, but they also conduct fund raising drives campus-wide at their schools to help pay for building materials. They pay for their meals while they are here. Often times they take over a local school gymnasium and simply put their sleeping bags on the floor. WorkFest is one of the most exciting and rewarding events at CAP. It's a win-win situation. Students go back to campus knowing that they have performed a vital service. Dozens of families sleep better at night because their homes are safer and warmer.

Chapter 13

Cliffie's Story continues
(death and a graveyard on the hill)

We were getting along fine until Vernon took sick in 1987. I was still sewing a lot of quilt tops and raising a big garden. I still sold a lot of shuck beans and other garden stuff. I hulled out black walnuts by the tub full and sold them. One year I had 128 quarts of walnut kernels. If you don't think that's much, try cracking out a cup-full yourself.

I still canned most of what we liked to eat. I put up green beans, beets, corn, sweet potatoes, pears, apples, peaches, kraut, pickles and so forth and I dried a lot of stuff too, especially beans and apples. We still grew pumpkins, potatoes, onions, turnips and so forth that would keep on their own through the winter. And what meat we ate came off the place too.

But when Vernon got unable to help with the livestock, I just could not take care of him and handle chores like I used to. We had two or three horses and a pair of mules, a few head of beef cattle and two milk cows but I was just not able to take care of them like they needed to be so I sold them all off. More than anything else, I hated to see my milk cows go and I miss them to this

Hand-carved replicas of old mountain tools by Cliffie.

day, but it had gotten to the point that you could buy milk cheaper than you could keep cows.

I bought an electric stove after we moved to this house but I wish I had my old wood-burning cook stove back. I don't care what anybody says, food cooks better and it tastes better when it's fixed on a fire. I guess it's because a little smoke gets in it.

I had taken up whittling or carving as some want to call it, in 1973 and people tell me I'm a pretty good hand at it. Like I told you before, I've always been pretty handy with a pocketknife. I figured out how to make chains with unbroken links from a solid piece of wood. I try to show people how I do it but most of them still can't figure it out. I sold a few of them through antique and gift shops and

Miniature chairs carved by Cliffie

gave away, I don't know how many, to special friends and relatives. I also carved wooden hammers, miniature furniture, little figurines out of walnuts and peach seeds, old farm stuff like plows and sleds.

Once I carved a small, wooden four-poster bed and my granddaughter took it to Lexington to enter in a craft fair where every thing had to be hand carved. But when it was juried they turned it down because they said the pieces had been turned on a lathe. I took that as a high compliment. I wouldn't know what to do with a lathe if I had one but they were right about the pieces being turned. They had been turned over and over a thousand times as I rounded them out

Miniature doll's bed carved by Cliffie

with my little knife. I have included several pictures of my carvings in this book and I keep a display case full at home to show off when people come to see me.

Vernon got sicker and needed attention pretty much around the clock and there was nobody here to help me with him. Then our road washed out so bad that a car couldn't get up it to take him to the doctor.

I called the county and one day they showed up with two loads of gravel to fix it. One of the men called in to tell the courthouse where they were and do you know, they turned around and took that gravel someplace else. I guess they thought I had voted the wrong way.

Vernon and Cliffie

So I packed rocks from anywhere I could find them and beat them in the road with a sledgehammer so that a car could get up it. I finally had to break down and buy a load of gravel from over in Jackson County. Anyway, before the next election the politician responsible for knocking me out of the gravel came up to the door all bright eyed and bushy tailed wanting to hug on me and wanting me to vote for him. To make a long story short I told him exactly what had happened. When he left here he was droopy eyed and his tail was between his legs.

Vernon died on the twenty fifth day of August in 1988. We had been married fifty-four years and almost six months. He was 82 years old. He and Jesse Darrell are buried in a little cemetery I've fenced off for the family on the point here behind my house. It will also be my final resting place and I hope that any of my offspring who want to rest on this old place will use it too.

Here's a little poem that I wrote for Vernon:

Ode To My Husband Vernon
By Cliffie Strong

I once was a lost rib from this man's side
And when he found me, I became his bride
For 54 years we loved each other
Four times I became a mother
First a daughter, then a son
Then another daughter and another son
That's the way it all begun
We worked very hard to make the food
That it took to feed our brood
But now he's gone to live with God
No more on this earth to trod
I plan to meet him one sweet day
Around God's throne is where we'll stay

After Vernon's death I was as lonely as a person can get and I was in the depths of despair. The one person who had been my constant companion, my equal partner in everything for all my adult life was gone from me. We were always pretty independent about the ways we performed our responsibilities but together we were one. You don't realize how much comfort and security there is in that until half of that oneness is gone. I had no idea how I was going to get along without him.

Chapter 14

CAP Counseling Services

Had Cliffie but known about it, CAP has a staff of professional counselors who would have helped her work through her grief and despair. Naomi or a CAP volunteer would gladly have transported her to the nearest counseling office. Grief, especially when it involves the death of a lifelong mate or family member, is often devastating and so overwhelming that people suffering from it lose sight of any direction in their lives.

"Where there is no counsel, the people fall: But in the multitude of counselors there is safety." Proverbs 11:14.

This Biblical quote has been featured prominently on the front cover of CAP's Family Life Counseling Service brochure that is placed in churches, courtrooms, juvenile centers, social service agencies and other places where emotionally hurting people may show up.

For nearly three decades CAP has recognized that professional behavioral and psychological counseling can frequently be the means whereby folks, literally at the end of despair, can learn to turn their lives around and return to healthy, productive lifestyles.

Suicide, on the one extreme, or life-time commitment to mental institutions or even long prison terms often result when ordinary people suddenly become saddled with horrible circumstances over which they have no control. Families break up when Dad has no job, or any prospects for one, and he often takes his anger and frustration out on Mom and the kids.

Families also break up, quite frequently, because one or another of the household begins abusing alcohol and drugs as a way to escape reality and often the victims of all this are the most innocent.

They are the sexually abused and emotionally devastated children or the bruised and battered spouses, all of whom have suffered physically and emotionally and lived through terror and horror that most people can't even imagine. They may even be the father or husband crying his eyes out, wallowing in a gutter of remorse and feeling as helpless as it is humanly possible to feel.

These are the victims and, ultimately, the results of a form of poverty not often mentioned in studies that talk about unemployment and low-wage statistics. However, poverty of the spirit is frequently much more devastating than that involving purely economic ramifications.

Without help, these victims often wind up in prison, or mental institutions, or they try to wend themselves through life carrying open mental wounds and functioning at a fraction of their real capacity. If they are youngsters, they fail in school and the cycle repeats itself. The ultimate alternative is that they take their own lives with a firearm or some other form of violence and frequently they take those they love along with them.

But, indeed, a high focus on spirituality is the pervasive culture of CAP's Family Life Counseling Service no matter with whom one speaks in its employ and this is no small operation. Professionally certified counselors and three administrative personnel staff the service in 13 counties. For practical purposes it operates as two programs, on one eastern edge of CAP's service area in Louisa, Kentucky and one on the western edge in Mount Vernon.

Members of the staff belong to numerous professional organizations and disciplines within their individual education and experiential backgrounds. Several also have church ministry backgrounds, have taught in public schools and universities and even had private practices. Counselors carry workloads of anywhere from thirty to as many as sixty participants each depending on the level of involvement they may need to have in any particular individual's life. In addition they frequently run group sessions for families, churches and other organizations. They also present seminars on such subjects as anger management, marital enrichment, domestic violence awareness/prevention and other behavioral issues.

The emphasis is on providing people with the tools and the processes to bring quality and wellness to their lives. The service even provides live Internet sessions for program participants who are too distant or too time-constrained to make it practical for regular visits to a Counseling Service office.

The staff is committed to the value of the individual, the importance of families, and the wisdom of spiritual values. Translated, that means counsel in dealing with abuse, parenting, anxiety, grief, family dysfunction, substance abuse, depression, divorce, guilt, stress management, neglect, anger, violence, and a host of other individual and family issues.

These issues are frequently compounded by

poverty. Almost none of the participants in the counseling program could afford to pay for conventional, private practice therapy and practically none of them have insurance. In fact, we don't even do third-party billing (to an insurance company, for example) because it has more work than counselors can handle just serving folks that have no other alternative.

The Counseling Service doesn't do any billing at all. Program participants (you will never hear a CAP Counselor refer to someone using the service as a "client") are asked to look over a sliding income scale and pay a suggested fee that starts out at one dollar per session for folks who have an income. Many participants aren't even at the one-dollar level.

Spirituality is an integral part of CAP's Counseling Services approach to therapy, just as it is vital in all other CAP programs. As Cliffie would say, many participants would tell you that the counselor who helped them turn their lives around was indeed, Heaven-sent.

Chapter 15

Cliffie's Story continues (God sends me an Angel)

Even though James Lloyd lived nearby, he wasn't able to help with much after Vernon died. In fact he needed much more in the way of assistance than I did. But he stayed with me at night for a while and I was so thankful for that. And my grandson, James Lloyd II helped me out a lot too with cutting wood and helping with other outside chores when he had time. The other three children and their families were all so far away and had responsibilities that they couldn't afford to quit so they couldn't help me much. I didn't feel like it was right to call a neighbor up to take me when I needed to go someplace but every once in a while somebody would offer to take me with them if they were going to town.

But I was still in a terrible position for an old woman to be in. I'd sit by myself and carve a while or I'd sit and piece quilt tops until my fingers couldn't take it anymore. I don't know how many

*Over 30 gallons of hand-cracked
black walnuts shelled by Cliffie*

thimbles I've worn the tips out of and they are awful hard to find in my size. I take a size 16 and the stores don't carry them that big because people who sew don't have fingers big as mine.

One winter I hulled out black walnuts until I had a washtub full of kernels and a five-gallon bucket full besides that. But it's still awful to sit in a house by yourself not knowing when you're ever going to get out or when you'll have someone to talk to.

I still raised my garden and I still do today. I grow cucumbers, sweet corn, beans, peas, tomatoes, green peppers, squash, onions, lettuce, turnips, mustard greens, potatoes and you name it. I have a few herbs and flowers all over my yard and around the edges. If it will grow in a garden and it's fit to eat, I'll tend it. So at least, during warm weather, right after Vernon died I had something to do and there's nothing like tending a garden to take your mind off of your troubles.

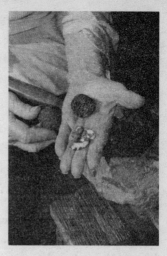

Cliffie holding a freshly cracked black walnut

I rode to Booneville with somebody to the second hand store which was run by The Christian Appalachian Project. It was called the Attic. There I first met my Angel, Naomi McIntosh, who was working in the store at the time. I knew Naomi was special the first time I met her. She is one of those people who just loves everybody.

One day she told me that CAP had an elderly program that was expanding to Owsley County and she was going to go to work for it. She explained that she could help me with transportation when I needed it and also get me out to little events and so forth. So Naomi started to come and see me pretty regular and she insisted that I call her when I needed to get out. She said she couldn't take any pay because CAP was paying her to help out the elderly who were stuck in situations like mine.

She took me shopping to the grocery store or the discount store when I needed to go. She took me to the Doctor's office. She took me to the drug store, the hospital, the bank and anywhere I needed to go.

She would set up little social events at Camp Andrew Jackson, which is also run by CAP. They have a big swimming pool and a lake with a deck you can fish from. They have a picnic shelter, and a place to make handcrafts and a big meeting room where you can sit around and talk. So she'd set up these meetings where us old people could get together and talk about old times or whatever else we wanted to do.

Every year at Christmas, she'd see to it that I got a big Christmas basket with a frying chicken or a ham or sometimes both. There would be fruit, several cans of vegetables, maybe a loaf of bread, something for dessert and anything else it took to fix a big meal.

There would always be some special little present like a pair of gloves, a toboggan or a scarf and so

*Cliffie Strong (seated on left) and her CAP angel
Naomi McIntosh (seated at far right)*

forth, but always something I needed and could put to good use. She told me that CAP fixed up baskets like that for over a thousand families every year. I just hope other people feel as special and thankful as I do when they bring mine.

She called regular to check on me whether I needed anything or not. And what amazes me is that she was doing the same service for about fifty other old people. Several of us would ride together with her at one time to go shopping and so forth, but that's still a lot of people for one person to have under their charge at one time.

God sent Naomi McIntosh into my life as sure as we are sitting here. She was my angel and I don't know whether I'd be on this earth today if God hadn't sent her. If she didn't save my life, she saved me from going crazy.

Naomi is retired now and in bad health herself. Over the last two or three years I've had other workers from CAP's Volunteer Program who are assigned to work with the elderly and I consider them Angels too, but they would not be helping me if Naomi hadn't discovered me first.

Now, I could sit here and talk for a month but I figure I've told you enough about my life in these old hills of home. It's really good to sit back and remember the old days and the times we had even if they were sometimes different than what we would have wanted. But if you truly have faith, I don't believe that God puts any burden on you that you can't handle until He decides to call you Home.

So that's about the end of the story I wanted to tell except for one last thing.

Just let me say this last word about the Christian Appalachian Project. First of all there's never been a program of any kind in our community that has done as much good work. I can't speak for everybody but I know for sure that CAP was Heaven sent to us old people. If I had a barrel of money I'd use it to pay them back for all they have done for me so that they can keep on helping other poor people after I am gone.

So I say thank you from the bottom of my heart to the Christian Appalachian Project. I hope that readers of my story will keep CAP in their prayers as I do every day.

May God bless and keep you all as well as He keeps me.

Signed:

Cliffie Strong

Cliffie Strong, January 20, 2004

Chapter 16

CAP's Elderly Program & Prescription Assistance

It is difficult to come up with a better explanation of CAP's Elderly Program than the glowing praise Cliffie has already provided.

However, Cliffie is not alone in being alone. Many hundreds of elderly citizens suffer the same desperation that Cliffie described when she lost Vernon. Yet making life better and easier for them is such an easy and simple thing to do. Basically all they seek is a bit of companionship and the knowledge that someone cares enough about them to see that their most basic needs are met.

CAP has, as we mentioned in the prologue, provided services to the elderly since its very early years. From the very beginning, CAP has believed that the future of Appalachia lies among its children. However, retaining the individual and collective wisdom among the region's senior citizens is crucial to any understanding of how to break the poverty cycle. As Cliffie has so eloquently pointed out, survival is hard work but it can be accomplished if you take advantages of every opportunity. CAP is specifically focused on creating those opportunities and/or teaching Appalachia's impoverished people how to take better advantage of the opportunities that already exist.

Helping people help themselves is, in fact, painstakingly hard work.

From time to time CAP has arranged for groups of elderly folks to visit and spend time in its child development centers. The magic that occurs when the very young and the very old are together is indescribable. Many young children never saw a grandparent. Conversely, many elderly folks hardly ever see their grandchildren. The smiles and laughter when they are together can be summed up in two words; pure joy.

Cliffie is fortunate to have an SSI medical card that pays for most of her prescription medicine. However thousands of elderly folks on borderline incomes simply can't afford the ever- rising costs of medicine. Many with serious illnesses suffer and do without. Others take inadequate dosages to make the medicine last longer. The net effect of such practice is that usually they get no benefit at all from their prescription.

A few years back, CAP discovered that most pharmaceutical companies are required to provide free medication to folks who absolutely can't afford to pay for it. We also learned that the process for acquiring free medication varied from company to company and that about the only thing they had in common was mind-boggling application and qualification procedures that most people would be unable to understand.

CAP employees have mastered these complicated application processes and work full time in the Prescription Assistance Program. They use computer databases that enable them to know which companies supply which medicines. They also maintain application forms and documentation requirements for each company on their computers and then assist low-income people in successfully completing the application package.

The results have been nothing short of phenomenal. At any given time the prescription program is assisting well over a thousand active patients and saving them, on average, more than $1,000 per person per year. Total savings to low-income patients totals more than $5 million. While the program concentrates mostly on elderly people because they are the ones more apt to need and qualify for prescription assistance, the service is available to any low-income family or individual who meets the qualifications.

The Christian Appalachian Project sincerely hopes that you have enjoyed Cliffie Strong's story. We are so proud and actually humble in publishing it and we hope that it has given you a deeper understanding and appreciation of central Appalachia.

Cliffie declares that her CAP worker is an angel. But we can say the same about this remarkable mountain woman.

While we only covered a few of our programs in the perspectives section, we also hope that you have learned a bit about our work and we, likewise, hope that you consider it important. We echo Cliffie's request that you include CAP in your prayers.

Finally, if you would like to know more about CAP, if you would like to volunteer, or if you would like to support us with a donation to help us build a better Appalachia, please peruse the forms on the following pages.

Please also visit our website: www.chrisapp.org, or call us at 1-866-270-4CAP (4227) and tell us what you need. Or simply write to us the old fashioned way:

Christian Appalachian Project
Development Department
PO Box 511
Lancaster KY 40444-0511

Angels of Appalachia

Please consider joining this special committed group of individuals who support the Christian Appalachian Project through monthly or quarterly gifts.

As part of this honored group, you will receive periodic updates about CAP's work in Appalachia. In addition, you will receive an Angel Pin signifying to the world your commitment to our programs. Finally, your name will be inscribed on our Honor Roll.

If you would like to join us, please complete the form below and we'll send you more information.

Name_____

Address _____

City State Zip _____

E-mail Address_____

Mail this form to:

Angels of Appalachia
Christian Appalachian Project
Development Office
PO Box 511
Lancaster, KY 40444-0511

1-866-270-4227

I am interested in volunteering with the Christian Appalachian Project

Please send me information on:

❑ One-year volunteer opportunities
   (year round admissions)

❑ Summer Camp volunteer opportunities
   (June – August)

❑ Short-term volunteer opportunities

❑ Group opportunities

Name_____

Address_____

City State Zip_____

E-mail Address_____

Please return this form or contact us at:

Christian Appalachian Project
Volunteer Recruitment
6550 South Ky. Rt. 321
PO Box 459
Hagerhill, KY 41222

E-mail: volunteer@chrisapp.org
Or call 1-800-755-5322

Dear Sue Sword,

❑ I am interested in helping to fulfill CAP's dreams for Appalachia. Please contact me in reference to planned and major giving opportunities.

❑ Please contact me to arrange for a visit from a CAP representative to my area.

❑ Please send me free literature about making planned gifts/charitable gift annuities, or including CAP in my estate planning.

❑ Please send me information about CAP's endowment fund.

Name_____

Address _____

City State Zip _____

E-mail Address_____

Mail this form to:
Major Gifts and Planned Giving
Christian Appalachian Project
Development Office
PO Box 511
Lancaster, KY 40444-0511

1-866-270-4227

Experience Appalachia...
Let the Mountain Spirit Take you There!

Feel the spirit of the Mountains in the people who dwell here, as you read their real life stories. See the impact of poverty in each photo. You will laugh, cry and be amazed by their courage and determination for a better life. You will see the hills of Appalachia come alive, and how you are making a difference in Appalachia.

The Mountain Spirit is published by The Christian Appalachian Project four times per year.

With your tax-deductible gift of $20.00 or more, we will deliver the mountains of Appalachia to your door. Your gift will not only keep you informed about CAP's work, but will help continue CAP's mission in Appalachia.

So, let us take you there.... simply fill out the order form below and return it, along with your gift, to the address listed below.

Please take a moment to help the people of Appalachia and soon you'll be able to experience Appalachia!

❏ Yes, I want to Experience Appalachia. I have enclosed a gift of: ❏ $20 ❏ $25 ❏ $35 ❏ $50 ❏ Other

*Gifts of $20.00 or more will receive an annual subscription to The Mountain Spirit.

Please Print

Name _____

Address _____

City State Zip _____

E-mail Address_____

Please return this form to:
The Mountain Spirit, Christian Appalachian Project
PO Box 511, Lancaster, KY 40444-0511